Bloomfield Twp. Public Library
1099 Lone Pine Road
Bloomfield Hills, MI 48302-2410

AMERICA'S INDUSTRIAL SOCIETY IN THE 19TH CENTURY™

America's Political Scandals in the Late 1800s

Boss Tweed and Tammany Hall

Corona Brezina

rosen central
Primary Source™

The Rosen Publishing Group, Inc., New York

Published in 2004 by The Rosen Publishing Group, Inc.
29 East 21st Street, New York, NY 10010

Library of Congress Cataloging-in-Publication Data

Brezina, Corona.
America's political scandals in the late 1800s: Boss Tweed and Tammany Hall/Corona Brezina.—1st ed.
    p. cm.—(America's industrial society in the 19th century)
Summary: Examines the actions of Boss Tweed, the powerful, influential, and corrupt public works commissioner for New York City from 1863–1871, and of the political organization that he and his associates controlled.
Includes bibliographical references and index.
ISBN 0-8239-4021-7 (library binding)
ISBN 0-8239-4275-9 (paperback)
6-pack ISBN 0-8239-4287-2
1. Tweed, William Marcy, 1823–1878—Juvenile literature. 2. Politicians—New York (State)—New York—Biography—Juvenile literature. 3. New York (N.Y.)—Politics and government—To 1898—Juvenile literature. 4. Tweed Ring—Juvenile literature. 5. Political corruption—New York (State)—New York—History—19th century—Juvenile literature. [1. Tweed, William Marcy, 1823–1878. 2. Tammany Hall. 3. Politicians. 4. Political corruption. 5. New York (N.Y.)—Politics and government—To 1898.]
I. Title.
F128.47.T96 B74 2003
974.7'1041'092—dc21
                                                                                    2002153977

Manufactured in the United States of America

On the cover: first row (from left to right): steamship docked at a landing; Tammany Hall on Election Night, 1859 (also shown enlarged); map showing U.S. railroad routes in 1883; detail of bank note, 1822, Bank of the Commonwealth of Kentucky; People's Party (Populist) Convention at Columbus, Nebraska, 1890; Republican ticket, 1865. Second row (from left to right): William McKinley gives a campaign speech in 1896; parade banner of the Veterans of the Haymarket Riot; Alexander Graham Bell's sketch of the telephone, c. 1876; public declaration of the government's ability to crush monopolies; city planners' illustration of Stockton, California; railroad construction camp, Nebraska, 1889.

Photo credits: cover, pp. 5, 8, 20, 24 © Library of Congress, Prints and Photographs Division; pp. 6, 17 © Hulton/Archive/Getty Images; pp. 10, 15, 27 © Bettmann/Corbis; pp. 16, 23 © Corbis; p. 26 © Library of Congress, Serial and Government Publications.

Designer: Tahara Hasan; **Editor:** Jill Jarnow

Contents

1
A Promising Young Man of New York

William M. Tweed was once the most powerful man in New York City. The mayor followed his orders. Powerful businessmen asked him for favors. People nicknamed him Boss Tweed.

Under Tweed, the city built new streets, museums, parks, and much more. He helped the poor. Immigrants became proud Americans.

But Tweed is not remembered for his good deeds. Tweed cheated the city and became rich. He controlled the city's finances. He and his friends stole millions of dollars. Today, many people still connect Tweed's name with political corruption.

Tweed was born on April 3, 1823. He grew up in New York City's Lower East Side. He began his political climb as a volunteer firefighter. Firemen were local celebrities.

The Tammany Tiger

Tweed was very proud of his fire company. He chose a snarling tiger as its mascot. The tiger followed him into power. It later came to stand for Tammany Hall. But Tweed's tiger turned against him. Thomas Nast used the tiger in his cartoons to represent the corruption of Tammany Hall.

The handsome young Tweed was very popular. At six feet tall, he stood out in a crowd. In 1850, Tweed became foreman of a new fire company.

That year, Tweed ran for public office. He wanted to be assistant alderman for his ward. His family was not happy. His father made furniture. He wanted his son to stay in the family business.

Aldermen served on the city council. They were very powerful. They granted saloon licenses and appointed policemen. The council decided who could run buses and ferries. It controlled city improvements. Members also served as judges in the mayor's court.

6

Tweed narrowly lost the election. But he ran again the next year. This time, he won. In 1851, Tweed became an alderman. This was his first political job.

At that time, many aldermen were dishonest. They often accepted bribes. In return, aldermen gave out favors. Bribes took many forms. Aldermen changed laws for money. They sold the rights to run ferries. An alderman's friend could buy a city job. Tweed followed their example.

Tweed purchased land for the city to use as a cemetery. It was worth only $30,000. He told the city he paid $103,450. The city council pocketed much of this amount.

In 1852, Tweed wanted a more important office. He ran for a seat in the House of Representatives in Washington, DC. He easily won. But Tweed did not like being a congressman in Washington. He made only one speech during his term. He didn't have much power. He missed New York and his buddies.

Tweed's term lasted two years. Meanwhile, he kept his post of alderman. He remained on the city council. But he

This photograph of politician William Marcy Tweed is from about 1865. He became known as Boss Tweed, head of New York City's notorious Tweed Ring. A political machine, the Tweed Ring ran New York City's politics and robbed the city of millions of dollars. Although Tweed never became mayor, he held more power than New York's mayor.

THE FORTY THIEVES OR THE COMMON SCOUNDRELS OF NEW-YORK.
Breaking up of a Grand Spree in the Tea Room & total abflustification of the common scoundrels.
For Sale at 124 Nassau St. N.Y.

In this political cartoon from 1840, the artist illustrates the corruption of the New York City Democrats, who were controlled by the politicians of Tammany Hall. This lithograph portrays drunken merriment as men make illegal business deals with each other. At the front of the scene is a huge, unsteady man who is meant to represent Boss Tweed.

decided not to run for reelection. The city council was in trouble. The public had learned of the aldermen's dishonesty. People called them the Forty Thieves. Reformers ran for their offices. They promised not to cheat the city. Many of Tweed's friends lost their offices.

2
Tammany Hall

Tweed returned to New York in 1854. It was a bitter homecoming. The city had moved on without him. He had spent all of his money in Washington. He tried to regain his seat as alderman, but a Know-Nothing candidate defeated him. People in the Know-Nothing Party disliked people who were immigrants and Catholics. During this time, many people had moved to New York from other countries. The Know-Nothing Party appealed to people in America who were afraid of change.

Tweed was a Democrat. He turned to Tammany Hall. Early Americans had formed the Tammany Society in 1789. It was named for a legendary Native American chief. It was a men's social club. Members relaxed there. They attended meetings and held parades. Members used Native American words for some of their titles. They called their leader the Grand Sachem. Their headquarters was called a wigwam.

The Tammany Society's founders were not interested in politics. But eventually, Tammany Hall grew out of the Tammany Society. Tammany Hall was a political organization. Its members belonged to the Democratic Party. When many Tammany politicians held office, Tammany Hall controlled the city government.

Tweed worked hard for Tammany Hall. He wanted to become a powerful leader. He made many friends. They would later support him as Boss Tweed.

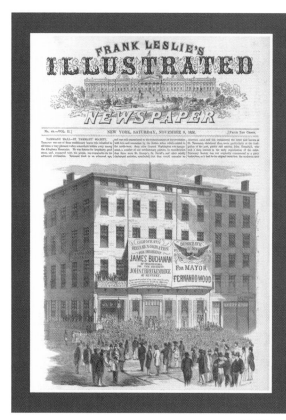

In this print, members of the Philadelphia Keystone Club gather for a reception at Tammany Hall in New York City on November 8, 1856. The club members are in town for the presidential campaign. Banners above the crowd announce that the Democratic candidate for president is James Buchanan and John Breckinridge is the candidate for vice president. Fernando Wood is running for mayor.

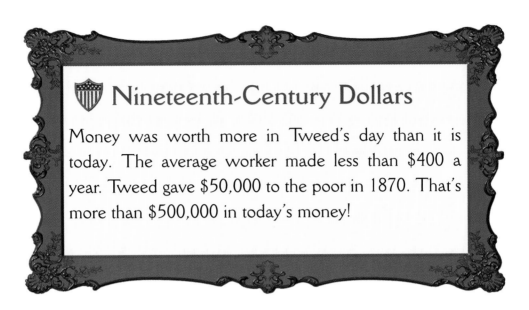

Nineteenth-Century Dollars

Money was worth more in Tweed's day than it is today. The average worker made less than $400 a year. Tweed gave $50,000 to the poor in 1870. That's more than $500,000 in today's money!

Tweed's fortunes soon changed. In 1855, he gained a seat on the board of education. He made it expensive to become a teacher. A teacher made only $300 a year. Tweed sometimes sold teaching jobs for $75!

For Tweed, 1857 was a good year. He made a lot of money through bribes. Most other Americans were having a hard time. The economy collapsed. People lost their jobs and homes.

Tweed gave money to feed the hungry families in his ward. He bought them coal. Later, people remembered Tweed's generosity. They recalled the harsh winter. Tweed's coal had heated their homes. People were happy to vote for Tweed. He seemed like such a good man.

In 1857, reformers tried to create an honest government. They made the board of supervisors very powerful. Only the mayor had more clout. Twelve men sat on the board. Half were Republicans and half were Democrats. Tweed became a supervisor. He easily foiled the reformers' plans. He would bribe, or pay off, Republicans. These people would then vote with the Democrats.

Meanwhile, Tweed's power continued to grow in Tammany Hall. He became a member of its general committee. He was now a Tammany Hall leader.

Tweed knew how to get his way. He controlled voting. Sometimes, Tammany Hall members disliked his choice of candidates. Tweed didn't listen to them. He would call only for votes in favor. He refused to hear any opposing votes. Then he would announce that his man had won.

His rivals once tried to hold a meeting. Tweed learned of their plans. He had the gas turned off in the building where they met. Back then, gas lit the lights. Tweed left his opponents in the dark!

3
Boss Tweed Takes Over

The Civil War began in 1861. That year, Tweed ran for sheriff. He threw all of his money into the campaign, but he lost. He was left bankrupt.

President Abraham Lincoln passed a draft act in 1863. The act said that the poor had to serve in the army. The rich could pay to be excused. People in New York City were furious. They rioted. Angry citizens destroyed buildings. A thousand people were killed. The army came to restore order.

One of Tweed's many friends was Judge George Barnard. He ruled that the draft act was unconstitutional. Tweed arranged to pay volunteer soldiers. He became very popular with New Yorkers.

In 1863, Tweed became Grand Sachem. He was now the most powerful leader in Tammany Hall. Voters trusted him. He gave important posts to his friends.

People respected him and called him Boss Tweed. Many men would have been satisfied, but Tweed wanted more.

The Civil War ended in 1865. The city now had to face its own issues. In 1830, less than 250,000 people lived in New York City. By 1860, the population had increased to 1,175,000. More than 300,000 people would move to the city in the next ten years.

New York City grew larger. People crowded into areas that had been nearly empty. The narrow streets were packed.The city had to build more streets. More people needed homes, schools, and offices. They required new sewers and public transportation.

Many of the new people were immigrants. They came from all over Europe. A wave of Irish and Germans arrived. Some immigrants did not speak English. They did not understand American laws or customs. Many had left their homes to escape poverty. They were poor when they arrived. Many native New Yorkers disliked them.

There were no government organizations to help immigrants. Private groups helped many newcomers. Many were religious groups. But they could not help everyone. Many immigrants didn't know where to turn.

Tweed saw the problems of the growing city and the immigrants. He liked immigrants. He helped them. He

This political cartoon from approximately 1870 criticizes the unsanitary conditions of New York City. Boss Tweed, depicted here, is welcoming a cholera epidemic. The artist is implying that Boss Tweed has allowed the city to become so filthy that he has made it vulnerable to disease.

gave many poor people city jobs. In return, he asked for their votes.

The city government made improvements that cost huge amounts of money. And Tweed controlled much of it.

Tweed had been penniless before the war. By its end, he was a millionaire. He gained most of his money dishonestly. He did not hold an important public office. Instead, he held many minor positions. He worked behind the scenes.

At the time, judges named people as lawyers. Lawyers did not need college degrees. Judge Barnard owed Tweed

favors. He declared Tweed a lawyer. People and companies paid him for legal advice. But Tweed gave out little advice. Rather, he used his clout in city hall to make things happen.

In 1865, his friend John T. Hoffman became mayor. He joined in Tweed's frauds. A few other men helped Tweed in his corruption. They would later be called the Tweed Ring.

Tweed controlled New York's city hall and Tammany Hall. The courts were on his side. But the state government dictated many city laws. Tweed wanted to change that. In 1867, he became a state senator.

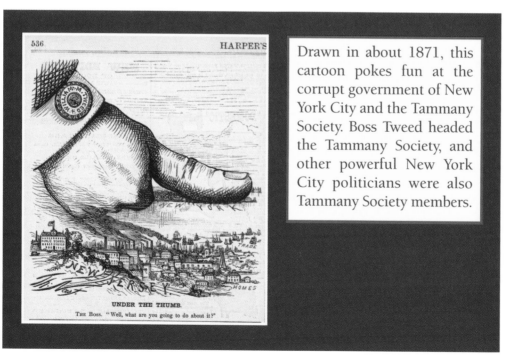

Drawn in about 1871, this cartoon pokes fun at the corrupt government of New York City and the Tammany Society. Boss Tweed headed the Tammany Society, and other powerful New York City politicians were also Tammany Society members.

Boss Tweed Takes Over

🛡 Living Large

Tweed gained weight over the years. When he tried to take a seat as senator in Albany, he couldn't fit in the chair! The senate soon realized that Tweed was remarkable in many ways.

After the election of 1871, Thomas Nast, one of America's finest political cartoonists, depicts Boss Tweed as a fallen emperor.

Most first-term senators had little power. Tweed quickly became the most important member. He proposed to give New York City more control over money. The state senate passed his bills.

4
The Tweed Ring
Rides High

An election in 1868 strengthened Tweed's authority. Some people call it the most crooked election in America's history. John T. Hoffman ran for governor. Tammany Hall spent $327,000 on the campaigns. Tweed turned to the immigrants. He helped them become citizens quickly so that they could vote. More than forty thousand immigrants became citizens in less than a month! In addition, some people cast votes more than a dozen times.

Hoffman became the governor of New York. Through him, Tweed gained even more control over state laws. In 1869, A. Oakey Hall became mayor of New York City. Hall's position and power would be important to the Tweed Ring. Many other Tammany politicians won elections. Tweed remained president of the board of supervisors.

The Tweed Ring used many scams to steal money. They were bold and creative. No deal could be too large or too small for profit. They did not believe that anyone could catch them.

Tweed began many city improvement projects. Workers submitted bills to the board of supervisors. They were told to pad the bills. This meant they would charge more for their services than they were worth. The workers took their fees. The Tweed Ring would split the rest. At first, they took 10 percent. But the ring grew greedier. Their cut eventually reached 65 percent. The ring took more money than the workers!

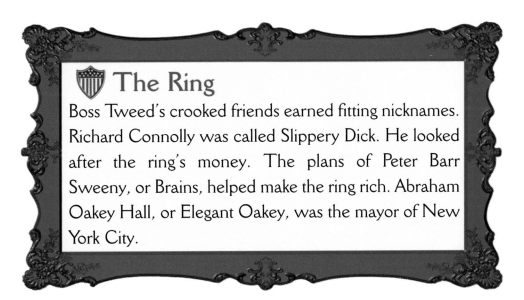

The Ring

Boss Tweed's crooked friends earned fitting nicknames. Richard Connolly was called Slippery Dick. He looked after the ring's money. The plans of Peter Barr Sweeny, or Brains, helped make the ring rich. Abraham Oakey Hall, or Elegant Oakey, was the mayor of New York City.

In this 1890 cartoon by Thomas Nast, the player holding the cards represents the taxpayer. The face of each king represents a primary member of the corrupt Tweed Ring. Boss Tweed is the King of Diamonds, Peter B. Sweeny is the King of Clubs, New York City mayor Abraham Oakey Hall is the King of Hearts, and Comptroller "Slippery Dick" Connolly is the King of Spades.

The ring also took bribes. They gave city contracts to the highest bidders. Businesses paid to have the laws written to benefit them. Tweed gave high-paying positions to his friends and family. He also gave jobs to the needy.

The ring's political favors were very valuable. The ring ruled the city.

Why didn't journalists unmask the ring? Tweed gave reporters so-called Christmas presents. He paid off newspaper editors. Politicians did not oppose him either. Many took part in the ring's theft. Even Republicans were guilty. Some helped to steal. Others were paid to keep silent.

Tweed lived like a king. He wore a diamond as big as a cherry. His family moved into a huge mansion. He was influential in business as well as government. Ring members owned stock in many successful corporations. They owned pieces of land all over the state. Tweed headed an opulent club in Connecticut. Members paid $1,000 to belong. The club's symbol was Tweed's tiger.

In 1870, Tweed proposed a new charter for New York City. The charter freed the city from state control. He gave out bribes to have it approved. The charter made it even easier for the Tweed Ring to steal money.

5
Boss Tweed Topples

Tweed seemed all-powerful. But trouble was already starting. New Yorkers heard rumors of city corruption. They did not care much. No one realized how much Tweed was stealing.

Then a new editor took over the *New York Times*. His name was George Jones. He challenged the ring. He asked questions. Why was the city in debt? How had Tweed and his friends grown so rich?

Tweed turned to the comptroller, Richard Connolly. The comptroller kept track of the city's finances. His books could reveal much of the ring's theft. When he showed some figures to a committee of businessmen, however, they did not find anything wrong! They said that the books were in good order.

Two other men joined the fight. Thomas Nast was a brilliant political cartoonist. His pen was cruel. He drew

This is a photograph of political cartoonist Thomas Nast in 1902. His drawings were considered pivotal in the downfall of Boss Tweed and his ring. In 1870, Nast began to create direct and harsh anti-Tweed cartoons, which appeared regularly in *Harper's Weekly Magazine*. When Tweed escaped from jail after being convicted and fled to Spain, he was caught because a Spanish immigration agent recognized him from Nast's portraits.

Tweed as enormously fat. The rest of the ring was pictured as shifty. His cartoons had labels and captions. These addressed the ring's dishonest deals.

Samuel Tilden was a democratic leader. He was also a member of Tammany Hall. He became Tweed's rival.

The ring fell in 1871. Its collapse began with the death of James Watson. Watson had been the ring's paymaster.

All the city's dishonest money passed through his hands. He died in a winter sleighing accident.

Matthew O'Rourke took his place. William Copeland joined him. They uncovered the ring's secrets. They copied down the crooked figures. James O'Brien, a former sheriff, took the figures to the newspapers. New Yorkers had ignored the *Times'* original attacks on the ring. Now the paper had proof. "Gigantic Frauds" read the headlines in 1871. People began to notice.

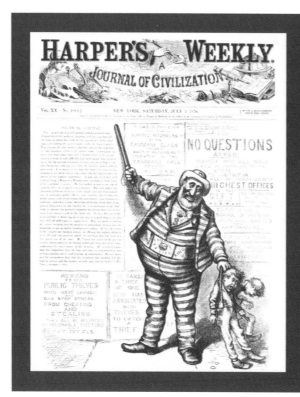

This 1876 cartoon by Thomas Nast appeared in the influential *Harper's Weekly Magazine*. The cartoon portrays Boss Tweed as both a convict and a policeman. With one hand, he holds two boys by the collar. In his other hand, he holds a policeman's club as he describes his scheme to manipulate an election so Samuel Tilden will become president and Tweed will become governor of the state of New York.

The most shocking news concerned Tweed's courthouse. It was supposed to cost $250,000 to build. The city eventually paid $13 million! Eleven thermometers cost $7,500. Plumbing and lights were nearly $1.5 million. Andrew Garvey received $531,594 for plastering. The *Times* named him the Prince of Plasterers.

The ring started to get nervous. Connolly offered Jones $5 million to drop the story. A banker offered to pay Nast $100,000. He said Nast could leave town and study art in Europe. Nast asked if he could have $200,000. The banker agreed. "Don't you think I could get $500,000 to make that trip?" Nast asked. Certainly he could. But Nast refused. He wanted the ring brought to justice.

The public demanded that the ring be punished. Ring members began to hide their money. Tweed's friends abandoned him. Judge Barnard ruled against him in court. The ring decided to blame Connolly for everything. Connolly then turned against them. He agreed to help Tilden.

Tweed won his race for senate that year. Most other Tammany Hall candidates lost. But Tweed never returned to Albany. On October 26, 1871, he was arrested.

Tweed went to prison. He created headlines when he escaped in 1876. He fled to Cuba. From there, he left for Spain. But a Spanish official recognized him. He had seen Nast's cartoons! Tweed was returned to jail. He died there in 1878.

The ring had put New York City deep into debt. Nobody knows exactly how much the ring members stole. It was at least $40 million. It could have been as much as $200 million. The city never regained the money.

Tweed's scandal left Tammany Hall disgraced. It recovered. Tammany Hall lasted into the twentieth century. Tweed was the first "boss" in politics. He was not the last. Many

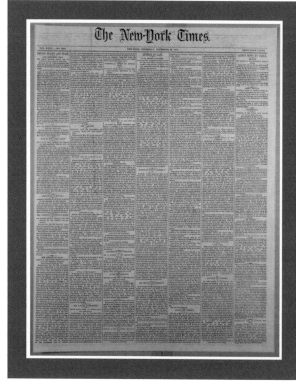

By 1873, luck had run out for Tweed and his associates. A rival managed to copy pages from the Tweed Ring's secret books, revealing how the ring operated. In November 1873, the New York Times began running editorials questioning how Tweed and his associates had become so wealthy. Eventually, Tweed was sentenced to twelve years in jail and fined $12,500. This New York Times article proclaims "Justice at last."

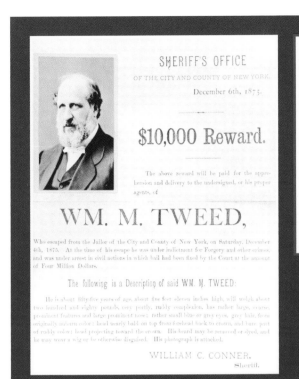

SHERIFF'S OFFICE
OF THE CITY AND COUNTY OF NEW YORK,

December 6th, 1875.

$10,000 Reward.

The above reward will be paid for the apprehension and delivery to the undersigned, or his proper agents, of

WM. M. TWEED,

Who escaped from the Jailor of the City and County of New York, on Saturday, December 4th, 1875. At the time of his escape he was under indictment for Forgery and other crimes, and was under arrest in civil actions in which bail had been fixed by the Court at the amount of Four Million Dollars.

The following is a Description of said WM. M. TWEED:

He is about fifty-five years of age, about five feet eleven inches high, will weigh about two hundred and eighty pounds, very portly, ruddy complexion, has rather large, coarse, prominent features and large prominent nose; rather small blue or grey eyes, grey hair, from originally auburn color; head nearly bald on top from forehead back to crown, and bare part of ruddy color; head projecting toward the crown. His beard may be removed or dyed, and he may wear a wig or be otherwise disguised. His photograph is attached.

WILLIAM C. CONNER,
Sheriff.

William M. Tweed served twelve months in a New York City jail before he managed to escape on December 4, 1875. This poster offers a $10,000 reward for his capture. Tweed eluded capture by traveling to Cuba and then to Spain, where he was finally caught. Tweed was escorted back to jail in the United States, where he died in 1878.

future politicians followed his lead and became corrupt. Bosses would rule in New York City and in other big cities for a long time.

Glossary

alderman (**ALL-dur-min**) A member of a town's or city's legislative body.

appoint (**uh-POYNT**) To name someone to a job.

bankrupt (**BANK-rupt**) Financially ruined; to lose or spend all one's money.

bill (**BIL**) A draft of a law proposed to Congress or any legislative body.

bribe (**BRYB**) Payment made to a person in a position of trust in exchange for favors or influence.

charter (**CHAR-tur**) An official agreement giving someone permission to do something.

clout (**KLOWT**) Influence or power.

comptroller (**komp-TROLL-uhr**) Person who maintains and audits financial affairs of a corporation or of a governmental body.

corruption (**kuh-RUP-shun**) Lack of integrity, or use of a position of trust for dishonest gain; crooked management of money.

foreman (**FOR-min**) A person who serves as the leader of a work crew.

fraud (**FRAWD**)   An act of deception intended to secure unfair or unlawful gain.

immigrant (**IH-muh-grint**)   A person who leaves one country to settle in another.

opulent (**OP-yoo-lent**)   Overly rich and fancy.

reformer (**rih-FORM-ur**)   One who wishes to correct evils, abuses, or errors.

scams (**SKAMZ**)   Tricks.

unconstitutional (**un-kon-stih-TOO-shun-ul**)   Contrary to what is written in the U.S. Constitution.

volunteer (**vah-lun-TEER**)   A person who gives his or her time without pay.

ward (**WARD**)   A division of a city or town.

Web Sites

Due to the changing nature of Internet links, the Rosen Publishing Group, Inc., has developed an online list of Web sites related to the subject of this book. This site is updated regularly. Please use this link to access the list:

http://www.rosenlinks.com/aistc/apsle

Primary Source Image List

Page 6: Photographic portrait of William Marcy Tweed circa 1865. Hulton Archive.

Page 8: Lithograph, 1840. Attributed to John L. Magee. Library of Congress.

Page 10: Wood engraving published in *Harper's New Monthly Magazine,* vol. 44, 1872. Library of Congress.

Page 15: Drawing circa 1870. Bettman/Corbis.

Page 16: Drawing circa 1871 from *Harper's New Monthly Magazine.* Corbis.

Page 17: Drawing from 1871 by Thomas Nast. Hulton/Archive/Getty Images.

Page 20: Drawing in India ink over pencil from August 30, 1890, by Thomas Nast. *The Illustrated American.* Library of Congress.

Page 23: Photographic portrait of Thomas Nast by Pirie MacDonald, 1902. Corbis.

Page 24: Illustration from 1876 by Thomas Nast, *Harper's Weekly Magazine.* Library of Congress.

Page 26: *New York Times* newspaper, November 20, 1873. Library of Congress.

Page 27: Poster issued by New York City sheriff. December 4, 1875. Corbis.

Index

About the Author

Corona Brezina, a graduate of Oberlin College, is a musician and writer living in Chicago.